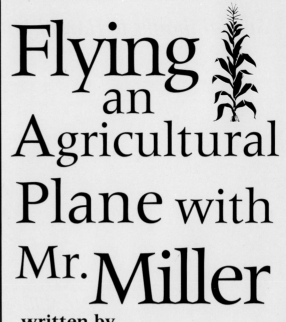

Flying an Agricultural Plane with Mr. Miller

written by
ALICE K. FLANAGAN

photographs by
ROMIE FLANAGAN

Reading Consultant
LINDA CORNWELL
Learning Resource Consultant
Indiana Department of Education

N7300B

CHILDREN'S PRESS® *A Division of Grolier Publishing*
New York • London • Hong Kong • Sydney • Danbury, Connecticut

Special thanks to Harold Miller for allowing us to tell his story.

*Mr. Miller would like to thank
Robert L. Mueller and Pat Schiffer for their help.*

Visit Children's Press® on the Internet at:
http://publishing.grolier.com

Library of Congress Cataloging-in-Publication Data
Flanagan, Alice K.
    Flying an agricultural plane with Mr. Miller / written by Alice K.
Flanagan ; photographs by Romie Flanagan ; reading consultant, Linda
Cornwell.
        p. cm. — (Our neighborhood)
    Summary: Provides details about various aspects of the work of an
air pilot who sprays the farmers' crops with pesticides.
    ISBN 0-516-21132-3 (lib.bdg.)   0-516-26468-0 (pbk.)
    1. Aerial spraying and dusting in agriculture—Juvenile literature. 2.
Pesticide applicators (Persons)—Juvenile literature. 3. Air pilots—
Juvenile literature. [1. Pesticides—Application. 2. Air pilots. 3.
Occupations.] I. Flanagan, Romie, ill. II. Title. III. Series: Our neigh-
borhood (New York, N.Y.)
S494.5.A3F58 1999
632'.94—dc21   98-7482
                                                   CIP
                                                   AC

Photographs ©: Romie Flanagan

© 1999 by Alice K. Flanagan and Romie Flanagan
Printed in the United States of America
1 2 3 4 5 6 7 8 9 10 R 08 07 06 05 04 03 02 01 00 99

Look at the bright, yellow airplane flying low in the sky. The pilot is Mr. Miller.

Mr. Miller is an agricultural pilot, or AG pilot. AG pilots help farmers. They use airplanes to spray chemicals on trees and crops. The chemicals make the plants grow better.

Some of the chemicals Mr. Miller uses kill insects and weeds. They also stop diseases from harming the plants.

Other chemicals make the soil better
and give plants the special food that
they need.

Mr. Miller has flown airplanes in
many parts of the world. He runs his
own business called Harold's Flying
Service.

Mr. Miller owns nine planes.
He keeps them in a large building
called a hangar.

When Mr. Miller is not flying the planes, he is fixing them.

During the summer, many farmers ask Mr. Miller to spray their fields. He is very busy.

Mr. Miller cannot spray all the fields himself. He hires pilots to work for him.

When Mr. Miller gets a call from
a farmer, he fills out a work order.

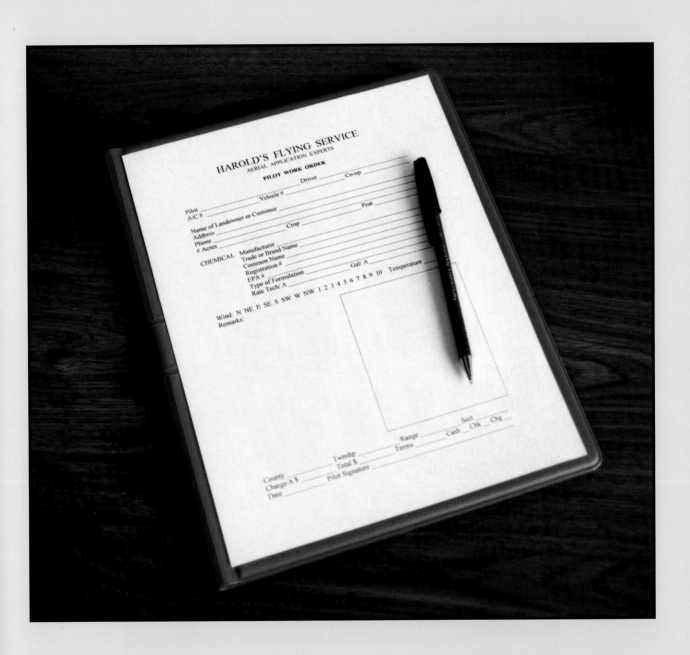

The order tells a pilot where
the farmer's fields are and what
chemicals to spray on them.

Mr. Miller's son prepares his father's plane. He puts the chemicals in a tank called a hopper.

Next, Mr. Miller's son fills the gas tank. On a full tank of gas, Mr. Miller can fly for two-and-a-half hours.

Before flying, Mr. Miller looks at a weather report. He will not fly if a storm is coming.

Next, Mr. Miller checks his plane well so it will run smoothly in the air.

Mr. Miller will fly the plane from the cockpit. In the cockpit, there is a radio and a computer. Sometimes there is also a telephone.

Mr. Miller wears a seat belt and a crash helmet when he flies. Sometimes, he also wears a fireproof suit.

21

When everything is ready, Mr. Miller lifts off and flies away!

Today, he sprays corn. Tomorrow, he might spray wheat, cotton, vegetables, fruit, or trees.

Mr. Miller sprays in the direction the wind blows so that the chemicals will land on the crops and not on him.

He does not fly close to tall buildings or telephone wires. And he will not spray chemicals if there are people below.

Mr. Miller learned to fly a plane
when he was eighteen years old.
He and his father went to the airport
together on Sunday afternoons.

Now, Mr. Miller's son flies airplanes, too. He learned how to fly in pilot school.

Later, Mr. Miller taught his son how to fly an AG plane and spray.

He used a special computer called a simulator.

He also spent many
hours with his son in
an AG plane.

Mr. Miller likes flying planes and helping farmers. He says, "There's nothing better than flying."

At the end of the day, he feels happy knowing that he has done a good job and saved a farmer's crops.

Meet the Author
and the Photographer

Alice and Romie Flanagan live in Chicago, Illinois, and have been involved in publishing for many years. Alice is a writer, and Romie is a photographer. As husband and wife, they enjoy working together closely. They hope their books help children learn about the people in their community and how their jobs affect the neighborhood.